Job Interviewing Strategies for Teens

Tips for Teens to Increase Chances of Getting Hired

Pamela Bodley

Copyright 2019
Published by Kindle Direct Publishing
An Amazon Company

Table of Contents

Clever Ways to Get Noticed in a Sea of Job Hunters 1

How to Make Your Dream Job a Reality 7

Ways to Prepare for a Job Interview - And Get Hired! 13

Drive Your Resume to the Top of the Pile Using the
    C.A.R.E Model 19

Get the Job: 10 Essential Interview Tips 25

Learn to Impress Your Job interviewer 29

Your Resume 35

What to Do When an Interviewer Asks You to
    Describe Yourself 41

3 Effective Ways to Find Unadvertised Job Openings 47

How to Ace That Last Minute Interview 51

A Teenager's Guide to Contacting Companies You
    Want to Work For 57

Simple and Quick Job Hunting Tips 63

Ways to Crack the Hidden Job Market 69

13 Simple Ways to Shake Off the Jitters Before a
    Job Interview 75

Getting the Job When You Have Limited to No Experience 81

Ace Your Next Job Interview by Listening Better 87

Dress the Part 93

5 Vital Qualifications Employers Seek in Applicants 105

Dealing with Rejection During Your Job Search 111

Learn to Handle Salary Discussions with Confidence 117

Steps to Take After You Get a Job Offer 121

4 Tough Job Interview Questions and How to Answer Them 125

Clever Ways to Get Noticed in a Sea of Job Hunters

Jumping into the pool of job hunters can be intimidating for teenagers! This is especially true if you have never looked for or had a job. You may feel like there are people out there with more experience and qualifications that you. The fact is that there are more experienced and qualified candidates than you, which is why you should follow these strategies to make yourself an even better candidate.

Getting yourself noticed in the midst of everyone else searching for a job can be tough. It sometimes makes you feel like you'll be searching forever, right? The reality is that there are a few things you can do to get the attention of potential employers.

Implement these three easy steps to increase your chances of being noticed:

- Include in your resume honest, but powerful, details about your work experience. Do some about the company and find out what's new and upcoming with them. Know *something* about the business.
- Understand how employers use keywords to narrow down their search. Keywords are buzz words in the job description that employers use to match up resumes with those same words. Ensure that your resume has the keywords that will get you noticed. Without those keywords, your resume might not get the attention it deserves.

- Be sure to list everything you did on your previous jobs if you've worked before! Don't leave anything out because that could be part of the requirement that they're looking for, so list everything you did in your resume.

Follow employers' social media pages. Although you feel like you're just one of thousands applying for a job at a specific employer, try following your desired employers on social media. Don't underestimate the value of that action! *Joining an employer's list of followers allows you a peek into the company and you can learn what's currently on their agenda or company bucket list which gives you a talking point should you land an interview.*

- **Be selective in the pages you follow.** Sure, you want to increase your chances of getting noticed, but it's a better idea to focus on companies that you really want to work for.
- When you follow pages, you're able to keep up on changes with the companies. You'll see developments, changes in leadership, and so on. This information keeps you current in the event you get called in for an interview.
- Linked In: Linked In is a professional networking website, but there is nothing saying that you, as a teen can't create a profile. Make your full profile viewable to employers. The last thing you want is

for an employer to be interested in you, but unable to see your full profile.

1. **Join online discussions with employers.** Take your interest in an employer one step further by joining discussions. *Many companies post discussion topics to get feedback from individuals in the industry.* Even if you don't comment, you can see what they're talking about, where their interests are and what topics, events or are relevant are relevant to them.

    - If you choose to comment, your worthwhile contribution to a discussion can help you stand out amongst your teen competitors. Ensure your points are well thought out and respectful. Potential employers will be impressed that you thought enough to engage them.
    - Remember to check your grammar and spelling. Yes, social media is more accepting of broken English and spelling errors, but remember you're job hunting! So no shortcut text message style comments. Use full words, spelled correctly and using the correct punctuation. Remember, you only have one time to make a first impression. Don't blow it with a misspelled word on an employer's social media page.
    - Participate in discussions as if you're in an interview. You have no idea who's reading your feedback, so make it good! Ask questions about

new products, services or ventures the company is involved in. Show an interest.

Remember that whatever is meant to be yours is there for the taking. ***Try not to feel intimidated by the crowd.*** Just patiently and cleverly find your way through it.

By taking these steps, you can increase your chances of being noticed by potential employers. Be ready, so you don't have to *get* ready! Then, when that day comes, you'll be able to make a great impression!

How to Make Your Dream Job a Reality

At some point in your teenage life, it's common to want to get your dream job, whatever that may be. No matter how great a job may seem, you may find yourself wishing that you were working somewhere better or doing something that you have been dreaming about.

The good news is that you *can* go out and make your dream job a reality! Whatever the field, **you can find a way to get a job that really interests you. Doing something you hate should not be an option. If you hate it, why subject yourself to it on a daily basis, which means you probably won't excel at it. So try to look for jobs in industries that excite you.**

By following these tips, you can be on your way to landing the job you want:

1. **Ask yourself, "What do I really *want* to do?"** What makes you happy? Start there. One of the best ways to achieve your dream job is to find something that you already enjoy doing and start your job search based on that. By doing this, the "work" won't feel so much like work, as it's something you're happy doing anyway.

    - The beauty is that you can now make money doing this. **There's no better feeling than knowing you get paid to do what you would do for fun!** In a nutshell, that's the concept of a true dream job.

2. **Break it down into steps.** Sometimes when looking at the big picture, it's easy to get overwhelmed and feel intimidated. By breaking it down into a series of smaller steps, it's less stressful and much easier to manage as you move forward.

   - *This will also boost your self-esteem and confidence.* You will feel a sense of pride in knowing that a step has been completed. The knowledge that you're actually going out and doing what you set out to do will also enhance the feeling of pride and confidence in yourself.

3. **Understand that you will be "entry level".** Some grunt work will be involved no matter what field you work in. Think of it as a sort of initiation rite. Even if it's a lower end job at the company you want to work for, *it still gets your foot in the door* and, in time, you can make your way up the ladder.

4. **Find a mentor.** Mentors can be very helpful when it comes to getting your dream job. *They achieve a dual purpose* of showing you the ropes and giving you the skills you need, while also acting as a great reference for when the big moment does come.

   - If you're having trouble finding a suitable mentor, a good role model or icon will work just as well. For example, if you wish to become a nurse, teacher or carpenter, try to follow in the footsteps people already working in these positions. Don't be afraid or embarrassed to ask for help. Adults will feel flattered that you are interested in their profession and if you show them that you are serious, they will likely be glad to help out.

5. **Ignore the pessimists.** Depending on the field you work in, there may be some negative feedback from other teens or members of your peer group, maybe even from friends and family. For example, if you want to write a novel or be a rapper, you may be asked what your "real" job is or you may be reminded about how unlikely it'll be that you'll land such a job. Put it all aside. Your dreams are *yours!*

- Remember that your goal *is* in the realm of possibility, even if it takes some work to break into the field. Books get published all the time and there are more than a few successful rappers.
- When situations like this come along, just remind yourself that it's what you want to do. **Think of the benefits you'll enjoy once you succeed.** In the case of aspiring novelists, you need to only remind yourself how exhilarating it'll be to have a copy of your book in hand! Getting published is really easy these days so don't get discouraged or allow others to discourage you. Stay focused and laser in on what it is *you* want to do.

While your dream job may be a challenge to acquire, it's very possible to reach it, no matter how hard it appears. If you put in the effort and follow a handful of simple guidelines, you can find yourself working the dream job you have always wanted.

Ways to Prepare for a Job Interview - And Get Hired!

Since entering into the working world, you've may have already been on some job interviews. In most cases, interviews take on a generic pattern that you may have become accustomed to now. However, every interview can still make you nervous and anxious about going. *It's important to practice some effective, job-winning strategies that can help you outshine your competition.*

Try these essential strategies to leave a positive impression on your potential employer and make you a candidate worth hiring:

1. **Study the company.** Usually, people preparing for a job interview do a little research on the basic history and operations of the company so they can show they're interested. *However, when it comes to standing out on a job interview, your research and knowledge should go a little further:*

    - Researching the company's website to find out what's new and what they're focused on. If they are launching a new product, learn as much as you can about it. If it's a new service, learn the benefits of the service and find something superior about it compared to their competitors. Show that you have done some homework on them. This shows initiative.
    - Finding out about the specific responsibilities that are required is also an important selling point for proving that you're the ideal candidate for the job.

- Take note of the company's organizational structure. Find out who the CEO or President is and read up on his bio which will tell you when he joined the company and what he did prior to joining. This might now come up on an interview, but it's still good information to have.

2. **Rehearse your interview responses.** Interviewers usually request that candidates for employment say a little about themselves during the interview. ***This could be your ticket to getting hired or your ticket out the door.*** Prepare a brief statement that effectively sells your abilities and strengths. However, try not to overdo it and don't stammer or ramble on and on. Employers can pick up on "fluff" very easily! That's why you have to practice, practice and then practice some more.

3. **Fine tune your resume.** A common mistake employment candidates make is filling their resumes with irrelevant information. Remember that the potential employer wants to see if you possess *relevant* experience that can contribute positively to their business. For instance, if you worked for *Burger King, Dollar General* and *Pizza Hut,* those jobs would all be relevant for a customer service position. ***Fine tune your resume and sell just your suitability for the job.***

4. **Adjust your focus.** *If the job you're applying for is your dream job, you may need to adjust your*

focus. Making it happen means being *and* thinking positively. No longer can your mindset talk you into negative thoughts. In order to show that you're the best, you need to claim that status by focusing on it.

5. **Dress for the occasion.** Remember your interview requires you to dress up a little to make a good impression. It doesn't matter if the employees are wearing jeans and tee shirts. You get to do that *after* you're hired, not before. **Not only do you have to act the part, but you also have to look the part.** Invest in an appropriate interview outfit that makes you look well groomed and put together. Let your appearance make the statement, "I'm the one your company needs!"

6. When waiting to be interviewed, do not be on your phone, texting, talking, listening to music or doing *anything.* Take any phone plugs out of your ears and never wear headphones to a job interview. When the person interviewing you comes to greet you, you are expected to be alert, prepared and ready to engage. Resist the temptation to take your phone out and remember to put it on mute or turn the ringer off. You don't want to have your phone's notifications going off and distracting you on your interview. It also just looks bad to the interviewer. Use self discipline to make sure that you don't create your own distractions so that you can be on your A game.

These simple yet effective tips will surely guarantee that you paint an impressive picture on your job interview. Your goal is to ensure you get hired and the smoothness with which you pull these tips off will determine the outcome of the interview. Go in confident, knowing you did some "homework" on the company and prepared to talk about yourself if asked. Preparation builds confidence!

Above all, it's essential that you're truthful about what you're offering and believe in it. It's very easy for people to paint themselves "as the perfect candidate." Don't over estimate your qualifications, abilities or experience, and never say you can "do it everything." No one can do everything. By saying this, it will make you appear unsure of your actual skill level or your contribution to the company. Therefore, what's important is that you present the *true* picture of yourself. Employers like organic honesty and not an overzealous personality that can "do it all". Most of all, smile and have enthusiasm about the position without being over the top.

Drive Your Resume to the Top of the Pile Using the C.A.R.E Model

There is still stiff competition for many entry level job openings, so you need a way to make *your* resume stand out in a sea of other teen candidates. **The CARE model is one proven technique that can help you get noticed by employers and show off your accomplishments to your best advantage.**

This guide is an explanation of the four elements of CARE and how to use this format to create a dazzling resume.

The Four Elements of CARE

Context. Describe the context. Begin by setting the stage for your story. Set out what jobs you've held and any relevant details, For instance, even if you have just had baby sitting or dog walking jobs, it still shows that you were reliable and responsible enough for people to trust and hire you things most precious to them. Provide your job title and the responsibilities you had.

Actions. Chronicle your actions. *Spell out precisely what you did to fulfill your job responsibilities.* You could recount how you solved a challenge while baby sitting or maybe came up with a solution to a problem while dog walking. Don't make it sound dull or unimportant. Potential employers will like your positive outlook and reflection on your past positions.

Resilience. Show your resilience….that a challenge in a past or present job did not stop you and that you were able to solve a problem on your own. Talk about how you stepped up to the challenge and took responsibility for solving a problem.

Execute. Show that you were able to executive your plan successfully. *Explain any obstacles you had to overcome and how you executed the plan on your own.* This will show the employers that you are a critical thinker, can think on your feet and are resourceful in coming up with a solution to a problem.

Additional Suggestions for Using CARE

Tell a compelling story. *Try reading your stories out loud* to test how interesting they might sound to a recruiter. Make your story interesting, vivid and concise.

Develop multiple examples. *If possible, include more than one CARE story for each position on your resume.* Recruiters will usually read a resume slightly longer than one page if they see the qualifications they're looking for. Remember not to ramble on and on. Hit the points and end the story.

Draw on all your experiences. Sometimes other areas of your life can provide useful stories. In addition to your past jobs (if you've worked before) think about what you've done through volunteer services, in high school or college, self employment, or other activities.

Remain relevant. Read job descriptions carefully so you can tailor the stories you use to each position. Keep your stories relevant and brief. Going on and on about details unnecessary to your point will only make the recruiter restless and throw the focus off of you. Remember, just hit the key points that are relevant to the position.

Start with the recent past. Always start with your most recent position first and work backwards. Employers are more interested in recent jobs.

However, if you have never had a job before, find other ways in your life that has shown that you are responsible enough to hold the job you are applying for. Don't be intimidated or embarrassed that you have not had a job yet. Everyone has to start somewhere, even the recruiter.

Focus your job search. If you get stumped when you try to come up with relevant CARE stories for a particular job, don't panic. Just stick to your basic job description and describe exactly what your responsibilities were. Sometimes, even if your qualifications don't match exactly or if you have never had a job before, your great attitude, personality and enthusiasm can land you the job.

Highlight awards and recognition. *Recognition by others is another strong selling point in your favor, especially if you have never worked before and this is your first job interview.* List any awards, commendations or certificates you received and talk about what you did to earn them if you have no work experience to speak of at your interview. Be proud but not cocky or arrogant. Show confidence with humility, so as not to be thought of as over confident.

Include your education and training. As a high school or college student, your education would be highlighted at the top of your resume. Most times, your education goes at the bottom, unless you have a Ph.D, You can also integrate your studies, major and any training into your CARE stories. Show how a course in economics or fluency in Spanish can be an asset to the company.

Get the Job:
10 Essential
Interview Tips

Top 10 Job Interview Tips

Have you been successful at getting interviews, but can't seem to get hired? It's a common issue among teens. A job interview is an unusual situation, and you probably don't have a lot of experience in that situation. Many people naturally shine in interviews, while others need practice to feel comfortable and not be so nervous. **Time and effort are all you need to become a master at job interviews.**

Job interviews can be tricky, because they're not something we do regularly. However, there are many things about a job interview that are easy to manage, provided you put in the time and effort to prepare yourself. You only get one chance at each open position, so make the most of it!

1. **Dress appropriately.** It's far better to be overdressed than underdressed. If you have a friend or family member that works with the company, you can gain some insight into how you should dress. Otherwise, play it safe and wear your best.

2. **Be on time.** Strive be neither too late nor too early. **Ten to fifteen minutes early is a good target.** Many companies will automatically decide not to hire you if you're late. Ensure that you give yourself enough time to arrive on time. Sit in your car around the corner if you arrive too early.

3. **Know the company.** What does the company produce or provide to its customers? How is the company doing? Is there any big news? Whom are its biggest competitors? How are the financials? What is the biggest challenge the company is facing? Understand the company culture.

4. **Understand what your potential boss needs.** What skills and qualities is your boss looking for? How can you present yourself as someone with those skills? **Imagine what your future boss needs and strive to be that person during your interview.**

5. **Practice your interview skills.** Interview skills are like any other skills: they require practice to develop fully. You can't expect to be good at something if you only do it once every five years. Find a knowledgeable friend and a book of interview questions and get to work. Practice more than once!

6. **Get a good night's sleep.** You'll feel and look better if you get a full night of rest. Your brain will also function better.

7. **Be prepared to discuss deficiencies on your resume.** Why did you only last for six months at Harry's Chicken Shack? Why weren't you employed for most of 2016? Be prepared to explain yourself. How did you use your off time?

8. **Know your weakness and how you're managing it.** Most interviews will ask a question related to "Tell me about a weakness of yours." **The key to handling this question is to explain how you're overcoming it.** You might say, "Well, I'm naturally not very organized, but I've developed a series of lists I use each day to ensure that I stay tidy and on track with my work."

9. **Have a few intelligent questions to ask.** Know enough about the company that you can ask a question or two. Also, know enough about the position that you can ask a question related to it.

10. **Remember to send a thank you note.** Generally, email or snail mail is fine. Thank your interviewer for their time and no more than one sentence of what you bring to the company, as a reminder. There are plenty of examples online. Choose one that seems fitting, tailor it to your situation, and use it. Do so within 24 hours.

Make the most of your interview by preparing as best you can. Find a friend and practice your interviewing skills. You might even record a video of yourself, so you can see how you come across. **Be prepared for the most likely questions** and ensure that you understand the company and the open position.

Leave nothing to chance. Practice, practice, practice.

Learn to Impress Your Job interviewer

1. **Clean up your social media presence.** *Over 90% of employers check the social media platforms of interview candidates.* Go through all of your social media pages, and remove unsavory, unflattering or otherwise potentially negative photos and posting that would turn off a potential employer.

    - Be aware that recent court rulings give employers the right to ask you to log into social media accounts and allow them to poke around your account. Setting the security preferences isn't enough. Get it all out of there.

2. **Be prepared for "Tell me about yourself."** Have your story ready to go. Avoid talking about your education and job history. Your interviewer can already see that information. Tell your basic story, focusing on the attributes that would make you valuable to their company. Remember, job interviews are not about you, it's about what you bring to the company. Keep it interesting and under two minutes.

    - Show that you're a real person, rather than just another cashier or clerk.

3. **Be on time.** Even one minute late for an interview is one minute too many. *By being late, you give the impression that you don't care, don't have control over your time, or don't respect the time of others.* Any lateness can destroy your opportunity.

- On the other hand, it looks ridiculous if you show up 45 minutes early. ***Ten minutes early is perfect.*** Plan for the worst and try to be 15 minutes early. You can always wait down the street until the appropriate time.

4. **Know your weaknesses.** The second most common question is "What are your weaknesses?" Avoid cliché answers like, "I try too hard" or "I care too much." Give an honest answer and follow up with the solution you've implemented.

    - "I struggle with engaging people and starting conversations, but I've started to attend more social events to increase my communication skills and be more sociable. "

5. **Get plenty of practice.** There are many books and websites with the most common interview questions. Practice answering them aloud. Record your answers and listen to them. How do you sound? Are your answers concise and professional? Do any of your responses send the wrong message or raise additional questions?

    - *More practice will result in you being more confident and relaxed at interview time.*

6. **Video record your practice sessions.** After you have your responses down pat, it's time to work on

your body language. Do some research on effective body language and give it your best shot. Your words may be saying one thing and your body language conveying something completely different. Record your practice sessions and review your mannerisms and physicality. Are you presenting yourself as a confident and competent future employee?

- ***The perfect verbal responses will fall flat if your body language is in direct contrast to what you are saying.*** Some experts believe your body language is the most important factor.

7. **Know the company.** Know the company's core business, primary products and competitors. You might find out through your research that you'd rather work somewhere else! You're also likely to be asked what you know about the company. Be prepared with a knowledgeable answer. Visit their website before your interview.

8. **Dress appropriately.** Males probably don't have to wear suits unless you are interviewing with a company or corporation. If you are interviewing with a fast food, restaurant or retail store, you should dress neatly in slacks or khakis and a button down shirt. Do not wear jeans. Females can wear appropriate business type dress or knee length skirt with a blouse. The key is to look clean, neat, and

professional. Ensure that your clothes fit properly. Even the finest clothes look frumpy if poorly fitted.

Job interviews can be stressful. You need or want the job, and the interview is often the final stage in the process. There's a lot riding on that conversation! ***Job interview skills can be learned by anyone willing to put in the effort.*** Become an expert at the job interview process and get the job!

Your Resume

Does Your Résumé Stand Out from the Crowd?

Job hunting is challenging these days. Employers are flooded with applications for every opening and may spend as little as ten seconds screening each résumé.

Here are some suggestions that can help your résumé stand out from the crowd and increase your chances that you get called in for an interview.

Formatting Your Résumé

- **Hit the highlights first.** *Put your most recent work experience on the top right after your name and contact information.* A brief and compelling summary of your qualifications and skills will get the reviewer' attention and display what you can do for the company on the basis of your credentials and accomplishments.

- **Err on the conservative side.** Take it easy on the formatting tricks. Use bold and italics sparingly so that the text is easy to read. A clean and professional appearance is usually the safest approach. **Try to keep your resume to one page.**

- **Be consistent.** Make your document easy to scan. Use a consistent layout that makes your résumé easy to follow and find all the important information at a glance like company names, dates, job titles and accomplishments.

Leave lots of white space. It's good to keep your résumé to one page but even better if you do that while maintaining normal margins and 12 point fonts. Use bullets and leave some space between lines to make your résumé more reader friendly.

Consider a combination format. If you are a high school student and have never had a job before, you can use a functional format in which you stress skills rather than your work history. Employers still want to see the conventional reverse chronology so try using both, in two different sections, to cover all your bases.

Be creative. Take the multimedia route. *Consider supplementing your traditional paper résumé with a video or other digital content.* Give people a link to your professional website or blog or use your LinkedIn Profile. LinkedIn is a professional networking site. If you do not have a LinkedIn Profile, create one.

Writing Your Résumé

Emphasize keywords. Read the job description carefully and integrate the keywords into your résumé. It is rare that an actually person is reading résumés. They are usually tracked and chosen automatically. *If your résumé gets screened by an automatic tracking system, this will help it rank higher and get selected.*

Customize your résumé for each opening. It's perfectly okay and acceptable to have more than one résumé. These days, the competitive job market favors customizing your résumé as much as possible to specific jobs. Try to adapt your résumé to the wording and requirements on the job description. There is significant information in the job description that will tell you the kind of candidate they're seeking, while still being authentic about your true identity.

Mention your accomplishments. *The contribution you made in previous jobs is likely to be the most important factor in helping you get your next job.* Focus on how you were able to learn the cash register quickly to move customers faster, how you won employee of the week, or any other awards, earned promotions or contributed ideas to help the business.

Use action words. As you're describing your accomplishments, try to start each bullet with a verb. This makes you sound more dynamic and makes your résumé more interesting to read.

Be concise. Try to pack lots of information into as few words as possible. Avoid any repetition or empty jargon. Keep your sentences short.

Proofread everything. Print out a copy of your résumé to proofread. Read it backwards word by word. Give it to at least one friend or family member because a fresh pair of eyes may spot typos that have become invisible to you.

The job market is tough, but a résumé that looks good and quickly demonstrates your strongest selling points could help you rise to the top of the stack. Give yourself the best chance to succeed by crafting a résumé that will make your prospective employer want to learn more about you.

What to Do When an Interviewer Asks You to Describe Yourself

"Tell me about yourself," is often the first question you hear at a job interview.

The hiring manager may be stalling because they haven't had time to study your resume or they may realize that open-ended questions are an effective way to identify candidates who can fit in and perform well. ***In any case, they're often deciding whether it's worth continuing the interview based on how you answer this seemingly casual ice-breaker.***

There's a lot at stake, but you can make the situation work to your advantage. Learn how to describe yourself quickly and compellingly so you can land more job offers. Know the difference between sounding cocky and being prideful or confident.

Welcoming the Question

Stand out from the crowd. While you may feel awkward talking about yourself, it's really a golden opportunity. ***Think of it as an invitation to tell your potential employer what you want them to know about you and what makes you unique. Remember, they may have had other interviews that day.*** You want to stand out ***in a good way.***

Look for openings to say why you'll be a good fit. When the interviewer is talking about the position, pay attention because you can use this information to identify and communicate your strengths and formulate questions. A good opening will prompt the interviewer to ask follow-up questions about areas where you shine.

Determine your fit. Remember that you're evaluating the company while they're screening you. Do you sense a connection with the interviewer, especially if they'll be your supervisor? Are they listening attentively or shuffling papers? Do they speak to you respectfully? Your initial rapport may suggest what your working relationship will be like.

Practice for real life. Most conversations are unstructured, so it can benefit you to learn how to sound articulate and make a good impression. Never use slang when on an interview. Practice communicating with others before an interview. Being unable to communicate will ruin your chances of being hired.

Answering the Question

Keep it professional. The interviewer is mostly interested in whether you can excel at the job and work well with the other team members. *Talk about your career aspirations and academic achievements rather than your family background and hobbies.*

Write out what you to say. The ideal response time is about one to two minutes. Developing a script enables you to check that you can cover each main point without sounding too long-winded.

Rehearse your answers. *Practicing your answers will help you to come across as prepared and confident.* You can practice in front of a mirror or recruit a friend or family member who can give you feedback.

Be flexible. It's also important to sound natural. Even if you've delivered your pitch 10 times, you want to sound fresh, prepared and engaging.

Customize your approach. Just like you tailor your resume and cover letter to each employer, you can adjust your self-description to fit the situation. Depending on the position, you may concentrate on your customer service skills or whatever skills and experience is needed for the position. Background research will help you determine what's appropriate.

Provide references. While it's essential to be able to talk about yourself, what others say about you is often even more influential. *Mention the achievements or compliments you've had from customers and colleagues.* You'll also be showing the interviewer that you work well with others and appreciate feedback.

Tell stories. You're more than a list of keywords. Share interesting anecdotes that will make the interviewer remember you in a positive light. But remember to keep your stories short and relevant.

Create interest. Your self-description is like a movie trailer or the first chapter of a novel. Instead of trying to cram in your whole life story, make the interviewer want to hear more.

Walk into your next job interview ready and eager to talk about yourself and why you're an outstanding candidate for the position. Focusing on the nexus between your strengths and the interviewer's needs will help you to find a job you'll love.

3 Effective Ways to Find Unadvertised Job Openings

For years, employment studies have suggested that 70 to 80% of job openings are unadvertised. Many experts believe that trend is growing even stronger due to social media and employee referral programs. Plus, **this hidden job market often contains the most attractive positions and the highest salaries.**

While cracking this market requires action on your part, it's a lot more rewarding than reading job boards and sitting by the phone. Try these proven techniques for discovering the best jobs.

1. Job Hunting Through Word of Mouth

Gather useful information and create mutual benefits through networking. Focus on helping others while you uncover leads.

- **Identify your targets.** Research the organizations that you want to work for. Look through LinkedIn profiles and company directories for the names of key staff members. *Ask your current contacts to introduce you to people they know.*

- **Search broadly.** You probably have more contacts than you think. Your piano teacher may have a friend who's hiring.

- **Attend events.** The internet can be fascinating, but it's easier to make a memorable impression when you're face to face. Mingle at monthly professional luncheons, happy hours, and awards ceremonies. You may even find out about new business ventures while you're chatting with other parents at your child's school play.

Rehearse your pitch. Prepare an intriguing introduction. Focus on the future and what kinds of opportunities you're looking for. *You can tell you're on the right track if others ask questions wanting to know more.*

2. Job Hunting Through Volunteering

Community service can fill in the gaps in your resume when you're unemployed. If you have a day job, use your leisure time to make connections outside of work. Volunteer work can add to your portfolio and give you success stories that will impress your next employer.

Research causes. There's bound to be a group that matches your passions, whether you care about animal welfare, healthcare or education. Believing in the cause will deepen your connection.

Define your role. Volunteers do much more than stuff envelopes. *Pick assignments that enable you to expand your job skills, launch a social media campaign, or help with a fundraising.*

Cultivate relationships. Strike up conversations with other volunteers and staff members. Depending on your activities, you may also have the chance to meet board members or interact with the public and press.

3. Walk-ins

If you are looking for a job, don't be afraid to simply walk into a retail store, restaurant or small business and ask if they are hiring. Be specific as to what type of job you are looking for and always leave a resume.

Develop your presentation. Practice what you will say when walking into a business in search of employment. Be confident and specific.

Collect testimonials also known as references. Enthusiastic references from previous employers will enhance your credibility. Ask your previous supervisor or a favorite teacher or guidance counselor for written feedback that you can use as a reference, as well as letters of recommendation that you can attach to your resume.

Consider all options. It can take time to find a new job. Consider volunteer work can offer great experience and could possibly lead to a job offer.

A clear strategy and consistent effort will transform you into an insider who can successfully navigate the hidden job market. Meaningful work provides greater life satisfaction, so network your way to a job that you will love.

How to Ace That Last Minute Interview

When you're searching for a job, it's important to be prepared for interviews that pop up at the last minute. You might apply for a position and get a call back right away. Be prepared. These steps will help you to make a good impression even when you have very little time to prepare.

Steps to Quickly Prepare for the Interview

Try to reschedule. Try to buy yourself more time. ***Ask if there's a later date or time when you can schedule your interview.*** A reasonable amount of notice will enable you to prepare and perform better. If you go ahead and accept that last minute interview, remain enthusiastic and make the best of the situation.

Review the job description. The job description is one of the most important documents to study before an interview. When possible, review the job description prior to any interview. If you have to, go back to the job board where you found the position and review it quickly before your interview.

Try to collect other information and materials. Find out the name or names of the person(s) who will be interviewing you. Will it be one person or a team of interviewers? Also, ask if they can suggest any other materials that would be valuable for you to bring with you.

Learn about the company beforehand. Do your research. When you're moving at a more leisurely pace, you should learn everything you can about the company you're interviewing with. ***When it is comes to last minute interviews, though, it's better to just focus on key tasks and assignments in the job description.***

Why the last-minute job interview? You may be able to discover what created the urgency for the interview. Maybe this is a position that the company wants to fill quickly. On the other hand, this could be their usual way of doing things. Either way, be as prepared as possible.

Preparing for the interview. Always plan to arrive no more than 10-15 minutes early. This is more than enough time. If you arrive too early, then the interviewer may feel pressure or concern that you are now sitting out there waiting. You may feel that it shows initiative and drive, but it could make the interviewer uncomfortable, especially if they have to pass you while you wait. On the other hand, there's nothing worse than being late for an interview or running in at the last minute.

Consider these tips:

- Allow ample travel time. You can't predict the traffic and you never know if your destination will

be difficult to locate. Consider viewing the location on *Google* maps so you can recognize the area and the location when you arrive. If you are driving during rush hour, make sure you give yourself enough time for any anticipated and unanticipated traffic or other delays.
- Consider taking public transportation or splurging on a cab, Uber or Lyft so you won't have to spend time searching for a parking space.
- If a friend can give you a ride, you can even rehearse on the way over.

Get a full night's sleep. A full night's rest will ensure that you look and feel more alert at your interview. Always avoid sacrificing any sleep. If you stay out late the night before, it may show in your appearance. You don't want to be yawning and looking exhausted on your interview. Get enough rest.

Try some quick exercises. Try to fit in a workout the morning of your interview. Run in place, do jumping jacks, sit ups or whatever gets your blood flowing. ***Physical activity gives you extra energy and reduces stress.***

Steps to Take Long in Advance of That Last-Minute Interview Request

Have your wardrobe ready. Dressing for an interview can be a snap. ***Always have several "interview***

outfits" ready to go. Keep your shoes polished and clothes pressed.

Know what to say. Practice your interviewing skills. *Rehearse how you are going to present your accomplishments so it sounds natural and genuine during the interview.* Then, choose which ones to discuss based on each individual job opportunity.

Try some "woo-sah" relaxation time. Searching for a job is hard work and can be a job in itself. Manage daily stress with effective techniques, such as meditating or listening to relaxing music.

Establish a support network. *The help of family, friends, and neighbors is invaluable when you are looking for a job.* Join a job club or start one of your own for extra support.

Eat well before your interview. A healthy diet will keep you fit on those hectic days when you spend all your time looking for work. For breakfast, try oatmeal. If your interview is in the afternoon try a simple salad of greens and spruce it up by adding some cheese or chicken.

It can be both challenging and nerve-racking when you receive a last minute interview. *Always stay a few steps ahead and have everything ready to go.*

Respond quickly and accept every interview that comes your way, even if it's at the last minute. If you decline an interview because it's at the last minute, you may not get called again. If the interview conflicts with something else, at the very least, ask to reschedule, but never decline. Remember that each interview brings you closer to landing the job you want.

A Teenager's Guide to Contacting Companies You Want to Work For

Searching for a job often means looking for who is hiring. You contact others in your network and browse through employment listings. However, you could also turn the process around and start looking at where you want to work regardless of if they are even hiring at the time.

Exploring these kinds of passive openings has advantages for you and your potential employer because you're targeting opportunities where you could do well. Find out how to identify businesses where you want to work, and how to communicate with them.

Learning About Your Preferred Companies

Use Social Media to your advantage. Gather information from the company website and LinkedIn. Introduce yourself on social media and strike up a conversation. **Check out GlassDoor.com to find out what current and former employees have to say.**

Read the news. Local press and industry publications can give you good information about the company. Maybe your potential employer sponsors community programs, or has other information that will help you understand what's going on in the company and what they may be doing in your community.

Do you know anyone working for the company? Ask your family and friends to see if they have any contacts who know employees at the companies you're researching. Personal introductions make it much easier to set up initial interviews. If you have a great reputation of being responsible and people have no problem referring you, ask someone you know to refer you.

Attend job fairs. Networking sessions and career fairs are an efficient way to access lots of information and meet prospective employers. Remember to dress as if you were going on an interview and bring fresh copies of your resume. Check the internet for job fairs in your area and sign up for updates on their website.

Volunteer your services. Do you want an inside look at the kind of work you're contemplating? Maybe you can intern or volunteer at the company or business. This may not be recommended for retail, fast food or restaurants, but if you live in an area with small business owners, you may be able to answer phones or do something that a business owner can't afford to pay but could use the help. You would be surprised at how any volunteer experience can lead to full time work elsewhere.

Identify the decision makers. Find out who you need to talk to by contacting the Human Resources Dept or walking in to speak to a manager of a retail or fast food place is completely acceptable.

Communication with Companies

Consider your contribution. Put the focus on what you can do for the company instead of talking about what you want. Talk about how you can add value and help them. Companies and businesses are interested in people who will help or enhance the business. Even as a teen, you have something to offer as long as you remember that it's not really about you on an interview. The business or company is interested in what you bring to the table, so talk about your strengths as it pertains to the job you want.

Hone your pitch. You'll need to capture their attention quickly once you make contact. Rehearse your pitch until you can deliver it in about 15 to 20 seconds. If you walk in and actually get to speak to someone, you may catch them at a busy time. You need to be able to deliver your "elevator pitch" in 20 seconds or under, hitting all the relevant points. Who you are, why you're there and what you want.

Send an email. Your first communication will usually be an email. Write a subject line that will pique their interest. Say you want to talk about their opening for a customer service rep and how you are great at helping customers have a great experience and want to come back. This is information that they will want to hear! Businesses thrive on return business, not just the one time customer. So, mentioning that you're great at customer service to keep the customers coming back should pique their interest and make them want to hear more.

Ask to meet. Don't be afraid to ask for the interview or at the very least, a phone call. Putting a voice to the person, makes it more personal for them. Also, they can hear how you sound, speak and present yourself. It's often easier to reach people if you call early in the morning or late in the day in the middle of the week. Be sure to leave no more than one or two voice mails so they won't feel harassed.

Build your qualifications. If you succeed at arranging a meeting, listen closely. *Find out what would make you a more attractive candidate and work on those skills.* Brush up on your high school Spanish or strengthen your social media presence with relevant content. Don't forget to scrub your social media pages of any unsavory photos or comments that could turn off potential employers.

Stay in touch. Remember that you're making progress even if your preferred company is unable to hire you immediately. It is okay to check in occasionally to let them know you're still interested.

Be patient. Landing a job can take time. *If one company fails to respond, don't despair, move on to other options.* Build a strong support network that will encourage you and give you constructive feedback. That can be your best friend, mother, father, sister, brother, friend or neighbor. Anyone who is positive and can offer you support. Stay away from nay sayers and negative thinkers. You may be dreaming bigger than them and they are not on your level of believing you can do it.

Finding a position you love will enhance your quality of life, and probably make your new employer glad you joined them. Make contacting companies you want to work for a priority in your job hunting. It will help your communication skills and build your confidence. ***Believe in yourself and think positively about your future!***

Simple and Quick Job Hunting Tips

Looking for a job as a teen, can be a bit stressful, but with proper planning, you can prepare yourself to land a job. It doesn't really matter what field you're looking to get in, there are universal traits you can develop to make you look attractive to your future employer.

You'll also benefit from making the whole process easier on yourself. Of course, you want to find a job as quickly as possible, but you also want to avoid stressing yourself out or feeling forced into making rash decisions just because you're anxious to find a job.

To be your best in a position, **hold out for a job that you'll enjoy**.

Consider some of these simple strategies for job hunting:

1. **Know what you're looking for.** Rather than searching for a random job, first do some heavy thinking about your talents and goals, strengths and weaknesses. What type of job do you feel you would enjoy and be good at doing?

    - You can even take a job assessment online to get some quick suggestions. These tests usually take your personality and temperament into account before matching you with a suitable job.

2. **Start networking.** Make connections with people who are already doing what you want to do. Maybe

a classmate, sibling, cousin or friend may have a job similar to the one you want. **Remember that the Internet is a powerful asset,** and you can develop your online identity to help you become attractive to employers. Also remember that the opposite is true, and you can turn off employers with the wrong images or comments, which they could possibly use to exclude you.

3. **Don't give up.** It's easy to give up hope, especially if you've already been out job hunting for a while. However, it's those people who persevere that succeed. Keep looking and developing your skills, because it'll pay off in the long run, even if you aren't seeing immediate results for your efforts. Hang in there!

4. **Strengthen your interviewing skills.** Try to know as much as you can about the job you're interviewing for, and go in with the right attitude. Read the job description thoroughly and understand what they want in from the candidate. Maintain a calm and relaxed demeanor and dress well to make a great first impression.

5. **Share your ideas.** You'll really stand out to your prospective employer if you *take charge and share your ideas* in addition to answering their questions. Well thought out ideas are always a great way to add value to your answers.

- Put some thought into offering a unique idea that can help the company serve its customers better, greater profits gain an advantage over their competitors. Since you're young, you see the world differently and may be able to offer valuable insight about possible future products or services. This will illustrate that you can think creatively and show that you've done your research into the company where you're interviewing and you know something about the company's core business.

6. **Keep your resume current.** Update your resume to highlight experience that can help you with the specific job for which you're applying. Your goal with any resume should be to still fill it with the information your interviewer needs. Don't forget to tailor your resume to the specific job. It is perfectly acceptable (and expected) to tweak your resume for different positions. Don't send out cookie cutter resumes for every position, unless of course, you don't have any work experience yet. Employers will notice it and probably won't call if you send out a resume heavy on being a cashier but the job is for stocking in a warehouse. Customize your resume to the job description.

- *Your chance to really shine is your interview,* but your resume should show that you have the skills to back it up. It'll also help to include keywords in your resume that pertain to your job description. In other words, use some of the same wording in your resume that is used in the job description, but don't copy and paste whole phrases and sentences.

7. **Diversify.** Continue to develop and strengthen the skills you have and add new ones as well. You never know when they'll come in handy. An employer loves a well-rounded employee.

- If you're interviewing for a sales position, the employer may like the fact that you also have skills in cashier and customer service.
- For instance, if you have access to a computer with PowerPoint, sit at the computer and teach yourself by clicking around. Knowing how to use PowerPoint is a fantastic skill to have whether your employer requires it or not.
- Also, watch YouTube videos to learn anything you're interested in to add new skills to your resume. YouTube is awesome for learning just about *anything*!

Most importantly, relax and be yourself. If you're fully prepared and patient, you'll eventually find the job that's right for you and fits your particular skill set.

Ways to Crack the Hidden Job Market

You can shorten your job hunt by knowing how to use methods other applicants usually miss. After all, if you're relying on want ads alone, you could spend a long time searching. **Advertised positions represent as little as 20% of total vacancies, and your resume often winds up in a pile with hundreds of other hopefuls.**

On the other hand, the hidden job market has a larger number of opportunities, and less competition. Learn how to position yourself to take advantage of openings that haven't been advertised. Contact small local businesses in your area to ask if they can use even some part time help. Offer to answer phones, file, open mail, whatever task that might help the business owner focus on what's important to grow their business.

Benefits of Cracking the Hidden Job Market

When you're targeting companies you want to work for, you're more likely to find a workplace where you'll fit in. That sense of belonging will add to your job satisfaction.

Receive more offers. The average job opening that's advertised attracts up to 250 resumes. Your odds of being hired increase when there are fewer candidates under consideration.

Cracking the Hidden Job Market with Networking

Again, make the internet work for you. The internet as a whole makes it easy to research and contact companies that interest you. Be sure to keep your profile updated because hiring managers may be looking for you too.

Reach out to local businesses. Many small, local businesses may need help but may not necessarily advertise on popular job boards like monster.com, indeed.com, careerbuilder.com, etc. That being said, this is where you can tap into the hidden job market by contacting these small businesses and offering your services (paid or not). By doing this, you reduce competition and may increase your chances Call up or visit a small business to inquire about their needs. ***Perhaps you can visit without your resume just to talk and introduce yourself first. If they are interested, tailor your resume to match the tasks that they need. Never lie about your experience. Simply highlight your relevant experience to what they said they needed.***

Volunteer your services. *Again, volunteering can't be stressed enough because it can give you additional skills and lead to job opportunities that you may not have found otherwise.* You never know who you will meet while volunteering. Use your skills to support a worthy cause. You can make new contacts and impress them with your reliability, attention to detail or ability to follow directions.

Join a job club. Your fellow job hunters often have valuable leads. Start a club or find one through community listings or your local library.

Attend events. Youth bureaus and networking sessions can help you connect with lots of contacts in a short time. See what's on the calendar at your local library or community center.

Seek referrals. Ask your contacts who else they would suggest for you to talk with. That way you can create a pipeline of information and resources.

Focus on giving. Remember that networking is more about giving than taking. Offer to help others before you ask for something for yourself.

Cracking the Hidden Job Market by Becoming an Insider

Complete an internship. If you excel at your summer position, you may have a shot at joining the staff. Pick a company with a track record for hiring interns and ask your supervisor for feedback to help you learn and grow.

Consider temporary or part-time positions. Even if you're looking for a permanent position, it may be worthwhile to accept temporary or part time jobs, especially if you're currently unemployed. That way you may be able to view internal listings on the company website, as well as network with employees who could have a say in hiring you.

Companies often bypass advertising to save money and target candidates who are more likely to match their needs. By tapping into the hidden job market, you can find hiring managers and the right job for you.

13 Simple Ways to Shake Off the Jitters Before a Job Interview

J ob interviews often stir up anxiety and nervousness. You're excited about the opportunity, but anxious about the impression that you'll make. A few simple steps can help you to feel more at ease.

Calming Your Mind

It's natural to feel anxious, but advantageous to keep it from showing. Looking relaxed helps you to appear confident and competent.

- **Take a deep breath.** Your breath affects your state of mind. Try calming your thoughts with three part breathing. Inhale deeply filling your lower abdomen, upper abdomen, and chest. Spend an equal amount of time exhaling.

- **Get enough rest.** It can be difficult to sleep before your interview, but your body needs to rest. Turn off the television and computers a couple of hours before you go to sleep and ensure your bedroom is dark. Read a boring book or take a warm bath to relax.

- **Eat breakfast.** Showing up to an interview hungry may make you feel irritable and who wants to have a grumbling stomach on an interview? Remember to leave time for a hearty breakfast that will leave you feeling energized and alert.

- **Enjoy the excitement.** Check your self talk. *Tell yourself you're excited rather than anxious.* Focus on the bright side. You are what you say you are. Stay positive!

Watch your body language. Gestures count too. Studies show that body language is 55% of communication, 38% is the tone of your voice, and 7% is the actual words you are speaking. Also, standing up straight and keeping your head raised will reassure you of your strength. Make eye contact, and work on your firm handshake.

Prepare for conversation. Take the pressure off by viewing your interview as a discussion rather than an interrogation. You're trying to find a good match that will benefit you and your potential employer. Essentially, you are interviewing them for a good fit also.

Preparing Your Case

One secret to building up your confidence is to walk into your interview secure in the knowledge that you're well prepared! Modern technology makes it easier than ever to learn about any company and its employees. Glassdoor.com can give you some insight on what current and former employees feel about the company.

Plan your route. Go over the directions twice to be sure you understand each step. Give yourself a little extra time to allow for traffic or public transportation delays.

Do your research. Browse through the website and scan for any current news about the company. Read the LinkedIn profiles for the staff members who will be interviewing you. Ask around your network to see if someone can introduce you to a contact who knows the company first-hand.

Practice your performance. *Recruit a friend to rehearse for your interview.* Offer to do the same for them. If you're on your own, practice in front of a mirror. Always maintain eye contact when answering interviewer's questions.

Dress the part. Lay out your clothes the night before so you know you have clean clothes that fit well and looks good on you. Males should wear a buttoned down shirt or polo shirt with slacks or khakis, not jeans. Wear shoes, not sneakers. Females should wear a suitable dress, skirt or pair of slacks with a blouse. Do not show cleavage. Have your shirt buttoned up appropriately just under the collarbone. Skirts and dresses should not be thigh high. Knee length or just above the knee is appropriate. Avoid miniskirts. Choose your accessories carefully. Style your hair so it stays out of your eyes and put on a friendly smile.

Listen carefully. While you're working on what to say, give equal time to listening. Listen to understand, then respond. Ask well thought out questions. Look for clues about what qualities the interviewer cares about and what needs they're trying to fill. **Remember that the interview is necessarily about you. It's about what you bring to the company or business.**

"Why should I hire you"? *This is the question that can make or break you. Let the interviewer know what makes you different from the other candidates.* Be specific about your background and strengths. Talk about how you can use them to create value for their company in the short and long term. **Never say you can do everything!** Focus on what tasks you do well as it pertains to the position. If you know you can do well but have not yet held a similar position, discuss what you would do in the position that would bring value to their customers or the business. At times, employers will be intrigued with the person who has a genuine enthusiasm for the position, than someone who may have had more experience but lacked passion,

It's a learning process. Finally, keep the situation in perspective. Each interview is a success when you consider it practice until you find a new opportunity. Rehearse your message and brush up on your presentation skills.

Say goodbye to sweaty palms and knocking knees. Show up for your interview ready and prepared. Rely on proven relaxation methods and careful preparation to help you land the job you want.

Getting the Job When You Have Limited to No Experience

Landing a job when you have limited or no experience has always been complicated because most employers want you to have experience already. Today, it's even more challenging because the requirements have become more demanding even for entry level work. But don't lose hope.

Traditional Strategies for Getting a Job with Limited Experience

Tap into your school resources. You can take steps now to enhance your future job search. Talk with your guidance counselor or the career services center at your campus if you are a college student. They may have additional resources and valuable suggestions for what you can do now to improve your future career prospects.

Showcase all your accomplishments. Review your victories in your life wherever they occurred. Do you get good grades, are you active in sports, the debate team or other activity that you excel in? Are you the neighborhood baby sitter or dog walker? These things may appear insignificant, but these activities show ambition, responsibility, drive, reliability and maturity. ***You have a track record even before you get your first paid position.***

Do volunteer work. (Yes, we're going here again). Volunteer work can help you make contacts, learn skills and demonstrate your community spirit, as well as helping a business who otherwise may not have been able to afford someone to do the work that you're doing. Choose a nonprofit organization with a cause that you care about and find out if you can create a niche for yourself. **Always remember to work just as hard as a volunteer as you would if you were being paid.**

Complete an internship. Internships are a great way to break into the workforce. *Many employers hire former interns* because they get to know you and value your contributions. **Put your best effort into being an intern as you would at a paid job.**

Seek part time jobs. Summer and after school work counts as experience. Find out if your local pizza parlor, local supermarket or deli needs a delivery person. To make it an even sweeter deal, you can propose to them that you would work just on tips for them to be able to offer this service to their customers.

Format your resume to your advantage. Employers will want to see your full background, so be sure to highlight your academic and extracurricular activities. If you have an impressive GPA, include that also.

Focus on transferrable skills. *Good employees are usually team players who can communicate well and solve problems.* Go into interviews prepared with stories that prove you've got what it takes. Be ready to discuss a problem and what you did to solve it. This shows the interviewer your problem solving abilities, as well as your ability to think on your feet under pressure.

Use referrals and testimonials. Ask key people to make introductions for you. Advance calls and testimonial letters will get your applications noticed.

Network like crazy. If no one knows you're looking for a job, how can they help? Take every opportunity to network and tell people that you are looking for work and what kind of position you're seeking. Be sure to follow up on promising leads, referrals and introductions.

Be honest. It's wise to make the most of your accomplishments, but avoid exaggerating. Interviewers can see through a candidate who is unrealistic about their accomplishments and achievements. State your experience accurately with a good attitude and a smile. Never think you can impress an interviewer by bragging about things you've never done or by saying you're good at everything. *Nobody* is good at everything. These mistakes can be costly.

Be willing to start at the bottom. Aim to get your foot in the door and be willing to start at an entry level. There are many other qualified candidates applying for the same position as you. You may be able to negotiate a higher salary later after you prove yourself to be a worthy employee.

Maintain a proper image. Dress for the position you aspire to hold. Never chew gum, answer and send text messages, wear headphones, smoke, swear or use slang on an interview. It is fine to show your personality but *ensure your conversation and humor are appropriate for the company culture.*

Innovative Strategies for Getting a Job With Limited Experience

Start an interesting blog topic. Writing skills are essential for many positions. Give employers a link to your blog. It's also a great opportunity to let them see your knowledge and insight, as well as your ability to write about and articulate it.

Take advantage of social media. Identify people you want to meet online via Linkedin.com and do some background research. You may already have connections that can help put you in touch.

Use search engine filters. Many job search engines have filters where you can sort jobs by the years of experience required. It's an easy way to save time and eliminate dead ends.

Hard work and strategic thinking can make your job search successful even when you have limited experience. Network, get creative and be persistent. We all have to start somewhere. Let these strategies help you sell your potential to a new employer. Don't give up and remember to believe in yourself.

Ace Your Next Job Interview by Listening Better

Active listening skills are a subtle but effective way to perform better on job interviews. *Half of all communication is listening but few of us get any training on doing it well.* Fortunately, listening well is relatively simple, and will become automatic once you practice the skills. Another key reminder is to listen to understand, not to respond. Many people listen only to prepare their response or rebuttal instead of listening to understand first, then prepare their answer based on their understanding. Strive for the latter, not the former.

Here are some techniques that will help you acquire more knowledge and make a better impression on your prospective employer.

How to Use Active Listening for Your Job Interview

Recognize your limitations. Many studies confirm that we only take in half of what we hear and we forget half of that by the next day. Becoming more attentive often takes some deliberate effort.

Relax your mind. Most people feel anxious about applying for a new job. Take time to quiet your mind and reduce distracting thoughts. Meditate, listen to music or read a good book.

Stay alert. Prevent fatigue from sabotaging your interview. Get a good night's sleep and squeeze in some light exercise beforehand. Sit up straight and dress in layers if it is winter. Being chilly makes concentration more difficult.

Show your enthusiasm. Successful people often enjoy talking about their achievements, especially when they have an appreciative audience. Make eye contact and speak clearly to your interviewer. *Let your positive feelings shine through when you describe your past accomplishments and how they relate to the position you're seeking.*

Reminder: Never, ever speak poorly or negatively about previous employers, supervisors or co-workers.

Position yourself as a good fit. *Use the information your interviewer provides to understanding the type of candidate they're after.* Explain how your background and skills can contribute to the position to become a valued team member.

Listen to understand. People listen much faster than they speak. Actively listen to each to all the information and each question offered by the interviewer. Take a few minutes to organize and collect your thoughts to give your response.

Keep an open mind. It pays to be flexible. Remain neutral to and don't reject a new viewpoint or job opportunity before you have a chance to consider it from all angles. Every job is different and may have different responsibilities.

Put yourself in your interviewer's shoes. Your interviewer may feel uncomfortable and/or nervous too. They may be under pressure to find and hire the right person by a certain deadline. Do your best to increase your chances of being that person.

Seek clarification. Avoid misunderstandings by asking for clarification on anything that's unclear to you. A good employer will appreciate your efforts to fully comprehend their expectations.

Ask thoughtful questions. Ask well thought out questions. If you need more information on dress code, hours, company culture or anything relevant to the position, don't be afraid to ask. Asking well thought out questions and showing a genuine interest in the position, can make you a strong candidate.

Meeting the Staff (if you're lucky)

Get to know the supervisor. The supervisor or manager will likely play a big role in your job satisfaction. *It is well known that people don't leave jobs, they leave managers.* Discuss the daily routine and responsibilities. Learn about their work style and how they establish priorities, delegate duties and what would be expected of you.

Pick up valuable information from co-workers. If possible, communicate with a few of the future co-workers. They can clue you in on the work environment and organizational culture. You can also use this time to discover who the best workers are so you can get an idea of what attitude, work ethic and skills are valued by the manager. Steer clear of employees who complain a lot, come in late, gossip or are insubordinate. Don't let their bad attitude drag you down.

Learn about the big picture from management. You may be trained by a manager or crew leader which gives you the opportunity to talk with some them about any questions or concerns you may have. Even if the time is brief, use those sessions to help get a better sense of the company's culture and what's important.

Go to your next job interview better prepared to listen. The session will probably be more productive for both you and the interviewer. And *even if you don't get this job, if you've kept your ears open and networked properly, you may have positioned yourself for a different one.* Active listening is one way to open up new job opportunities and build a better future.

Dress the Part

Like many new job seekers, you may think that looking good on paper is all it takes to get hired - especially with Internet applications becoming the norm - but *the way you present yourself to potential employers when you meet them largely affects whether or not you get the job.*

Yes, a firm handshake is necessary, but it's only a start. In order to increase your chances for a successful interview, *you must dress the part for job you want.*

Follow these steps to dress for the interview and beyond:

1. **Modesty is preferred.** While it may be okay to wear a low cut V-neck to a night out on the town, it's far from appropriate attire for the workplace. Practice modesty. You'll impress your potential employer and ensure that they feel comfortable interviewing you.

    - Don't wear anything that is too low cut or too tight. Your blouse should show not show cleavage, and your skirt should hit at your knee or just below. It's okay to wear a skirt without panty hose in the warm months, but *it's wise to cover up for a more polished look.*

2. **When in doubt, overdress.** If your coworkers wear casual attire, that's their choice. However, to stand out in a good way, dress slightly better than your coworkers on the job. This doesn't mean designer clothes. It means don't get sloppy in your

attire or get too casual because "everybody else is doing it." If possible, **take note of what management wears and try to style your clothing according to their style.**

- If you look well put together and perform your job well, you'll be treated accordingly. If your attire is always on point and you are neatly dressed with style, management are more likely to notice you, especially if you perform well. If you dress well but continue to come in late, call out or be disrespectful to your supervisor or coworkers, how you dress won't matter. In turn, you'll be in a favorable position with management which is where you want to be so you can be considered for a full time position if your job is temporary or for the summer or holidays.

- **Ensure that both the quality of your work and your appearance are excellent in order to fast track your reputation as a good worker.**

3. **Wear the right shoes.** Depending on the job you're interviewing for, females should wear a comfortable shoe based on the work you will be doing. Males should always wear shoes on an interview. Sneakers are way too informal. Some jobs may allow you to wear sneakers based on what your position will be, while others might require you to wear sensible shoes. Check with management to

confirm what the dress code is so you will be in step with everyone else.

- If by chance, you find a job in an office, low heels that are considered appropriate. But, *avoid shoes that go over the 3.0." mark in all office environments. Maintain a youthful but age appropriate appearance.*

- Solid colors are standard. Avoid patterned, bold colors and glittery shoes with all of the bells and whistles. As with any other attire, conservative is best. Males should wear a polo shirt and slacks or a button down shirt and slacks, with shoes.

4. **Proper grooming.** When entering a workplace for an interview, you must look like a professional. Therefore, your hair should be well combed and tamed, your fingernails should be clean and well groomed, and body odor should be under control. No, seriously.

   - **Males:** Get a haircut and maintain your hair every morning before work. *Shave your face if you have facial hair* and ensure that your hands and fingernails are clean. *Cover up any tattoos.*
   - **Females:** If you choose to wear your hair out, make sure it is clean and worn off the face, although a high ponytail or bun gives a neater look. And of course, *if you wear makeup, less*

is more. Don't overdo the eye shadow or blush. Cover up any tattoos.

If you want the interviewer to take you seriously, **your attire must show them you're worthy enough to one day be in their shoes.** When in doubt, overdress and dress conservatively. When your dress is appropriate and your work is top-notch, you're sure to get noticed as a great candidate for all the right reasons.

How to Ace a Phone Interview

Sometimes, potential employers want to pre-interview you by phone before they invite you in for an in person interview. Performing well on a phone interview can help you move forward towards meeting in person. Some companies are using phone interviews to screen large pools of qualified candidates. The fact that they contacted you at all means that there was something about your resume that got their attention. They will probably coordinate a good time for you when you're available.

- Choose a time where there is no background noise, like traffic, dogs barking or screaming kids, so you can focus.
- Be sure to have a copy of your resume in front of you so you can refer to it, as they will surely have a copy in front of them.

Here are some tips to make a good impression throughout the whole process.

Before the Phone Interview:

1. **Provide accurate contact information on your resume.** Let potential employers know the easiest way to contact you. Suggest that you can best be reached at home because of school hours. More and more companies do phone interviews without any advance notice so do what you can to establish the

best conditions. If they do contact you at an inopportune time, express genuine interest in speaking with them and try to negotiate a time that's better for you.

2. **Keep a contact log.** If you're sending out multiple applications, keep a contact log so you can keep them straight. You'll be better prepared for impromptu phone interviews or any return calls if you know which company and position they're calling about.

3. **Do your research.** *A phone interview requires just as much preparation as the face-to-face version.* Learn all you can about the company, position and people you're going to interview with on the interview. You may be able to find the interviewer on LinkedIn.com or on the company website.

4. **Listen to the interviewer, but prepare your responses and ask questions.** Jot down follow-up questions that you can ask while the interviewer is telling you about the position. It will help you sound prepared and make it easier to remember things you may want to address.

5. **Warm up your voice.** *Your voice matters even more when your body language and facial expressions aren't visible.* People can "hear your mood" over the phone. If you have ever gotten a

customer service person on the phone and they sound rude or you can tell that they are not smiling or happy to assist you, that's what I mean.

- If your voice lacks enthusiasm or a real interest in the position, don't expect to be invited in for an in-person interview. They will simply end the call and move on to the next person on their list.
- If the call is going well and you feel like it's wrapping up, go ahead and ask if you can come in and interview in person. They will either schedule you or tell you that you'll hear from them. But don't be afraid to ask.

6. **Ignore distractions.** While you are on your phone interview, let other calls go to voicemail. Ask your family or friends not to interrupt you if they are around. Give the call your full attention.

During the Phone Interview:

- **Be friendly and enthusiastic. Have a copy of your resume in front of you.** Make a strong first impression. Smile and hold your head up. Focus on the positive aspects of the position so you'll sound excited to discuss it.

- **Write down the interviewer's name.** It'll come in handy if you meet them for an in-person interview.

People like it when you remember their names, especially interviewers.

- **Be ready.** Be yourself and try to be relaxed and confident without being cocky. Some employers may just ask a few preliminary questions like "are you still interested?" or "when can you come in?" while others will go into great depths about your prior experience. Either way, be ready.

- **Be ready to talk about yourself.** You should have a brief statement prepared about why you think you're the right candidate. It should be about 20-30 seconds long. Never, ever talk about money! Never say you need it; never say that's the reason you want the job. Remember that the interview is not actually about *you*, it's more about filling a need for the company. They need an employee who can do XYZ.

- You need to be prepared to describe how well you can do XYZ and give examples.

- If you have never had a job and this would be your first job, describe your understanding of how important XYZ is to customers and how doing and outstanding job with XYZ will help customers feel valued and keep returning. Even though you've never actually done XYZ, you want to show a fundamental understanding of why it's important. This is just an example but you get the idea.

- **Avoid interrupting.** It can be difficult to know when someone is done speaking when you can't see them. Pause for a second before replying to avoid any awkward interruptions. Phone interviews are not meant to be long so the interviewer is probably calling to see if you are still interested and available, They likely have a long list of candidates, so considerate yourself lucky if a potential employer contacts you by phone or email. Use this opportunity to get the in-person interview where offers are made.

- **Request feedback.** If you sense any weak areas (like lack of experience) during the phone interview, try to highlight your understanding of them. Ask the interviewer to clarify their needs so you can offer more information to strengthen your case.

- **Ask questions that show you're a good fit for the position.** Ask questions that demonstrate that you've done your research. It will show that you're really interested in the position and give you another chance to talk about why you'd be an asset. For instance, if it a manager from a fast food business calling, you can say how you enjoy serving customers and how great you are at upselling other items. Up selling is when you recommend an item that the customer did not order. For instance, a customer orders a burger and chocolate shake. You would up sell them by offering fries or an apple pie, etc.

- **Clarify the next steps.** Ask about their hiring process. They may want to schedule an in-person interview immediately or let you know when they'll decide on the remaining finalists.

After the Phone Interview:

1. **Send a thank you note.** Send a brief note of thanks by email or regular mail. It's good etiquette and yet another chance to show you'd make a good employee. It doesn't need to be a long email; just a short note thanking them for the interview. Don't forget to express that you are very interested in the position.

2. **Plan to follow up.** Hiring decisions often take longer than expected. Most teens and young adults will sit around and wait for the employer to call and when they don't, they do nothing. Follow up in two weeks if you have not heard anything. Send an email because it's less intrusive than a phone call. Use tactful persistence without being harassing.

Phone interviews now play an important role in the hiring process. *Learning the techniques to ace a phone interview will give you a big advantage in your job search.*

5 Vital Qualifications Employers Seek in Applicants

Sometimes, it may feel as if the odds are against you when applying for a job as a teen. While it's true that you're likely up against stiff competition when interviewing for a position, know that there is a place for you in the workforce.

Employers seek five vital qualifications when fulfilling their position. **Develop these five characteristics within yourself to dramatically increase your chances having a successful job interview that leads to a job offer:**

1. **Diligence.** Your potential employer needs to know that you're thorough, reliable, hardworking and trustworthy. Employers want to know that they're getting their money's worth from the salary that they're paying you.

    - It's an employer's right to seek diligence in his employees. Whether you're being offered a position that pays $10 per hour or $100,000 per year, *you need to bring everything you've got to the table!*

2. **Maturity.** Employers seek a certain level of maturity in their young employees because it gives them peace of mind that they're making the right choice. You should dress appropriately, carry yourself with confidence and be ready to perform your job to the best of your ability.

    - *A friendly demeanor goes a long way.* A friendly demeanor, firm handshake, good eye contact and a great resume just may get you the job. When you display a pleasant demeanor, you give interviewers the comfort of knowing that they're making the right decision and that there's a good chance you will work well with co-workers and customers.

- Many employers promote within the company. If you lack a friendly, even temperament, you'll likely be overlooked because interviewers will see little potential for your advancement in the company's growth, culture or morale.

3. **Dedication to success.** The ideal employee is willing to go above and beyond to attain success for themselves and the greater good of the company. And, if the mountain is immovable, they'll willingly climb over the mountain to get things done.

    - The perfect way to showcase to an employer that you're dedicated to achieving success is to bring references from your previous employers, co-workers, and teachers.
    - *Be prepared to talk about your successes.* Explain how you went above and beyond the call of your job and give them ideas as to how you can do the same for them.

4. **Experience.** In any job market, experience sells. Sure, **a recent high school or college graduate can provide a sense of excitement and a new spin on the ordinary.** However, unless you're

vying for a job in a creative environment that thrives on new ideas, this is of little use to the employer. In addition, new grads must endure a learning curve, and that learning curve will cost the employer money.

- Even an experienced employee will need to be trained to do the job but because they have experience, they are prepared to handle potentially sticky situations. ***An experienced employee can save employers money and also begin bringing in revenue almost immediately because they already have some idea about what the position entails. But don't be intimidated by that. Plenty of businesses hire newbies understanding that you have to start somewhere.***

- ***The Catch-22.*** The number one problem that teens have is they can't get a job without experience and they can't get experience without a job. We've all been there, but don't worry, someone will give you a shot if you present yourself correctly.

- Even if you've just graduated, show the interviewer how your experiences can benefit the position and ultimately the business.

5. **Education.** If you are in high school, understand that you have quite a bit of competition in the job market. A college education is almost a requirement

in a competitive job market. However, most teens take positions in fast food, supermarkets and convenience store chains like *CVS* and *Walgreens*.

- If you are in college or your college education is lower than a bachelor's degree, consider attending an online or community college in order to obtain your bachelor's degree to remain competitive.

Even as a teen, you deserve to be paid a fair salary for your work, which in most cases will be minimum wage at first. And, in turn, your employer deserves to hire a qualified candidate.

Dealing with Rejection During Your Job Search

As a teen, you may encounter more rejections than you'd like during your job search. But don't be discouraged. Keep your search on track by following these tips.

How to Cope with Rejection When Job Searching

- **Face your feelings.** Getting turned down may trigger difficult emotions such as anger or futility. Figure out what troubles you most. It might be lack of preparation, confidence, perseverance or doubts about your abilities. This will guide you to the individual solutions you need.

- **Seek support.** Talk to trusted family members, siblings, teachers or friends. You may find guidance and support that will keep you motivated and focused. Job searching is not easy and it takes time. **Let family and friends know exactly how they can help you.** Find strength in connecting with people you trust and asking for advice.

- **Self Talk and Speak Affirmations.** Never beat yourself up metaphorically speaking. Don't convince yourself that you are not worthy of a job or that others are better or smarter than you. That is simply not true. Tell yourself, you are smart, you are worthy, you are competent, you are responsible. **Saying these words are powerful!** Say them every morning in the shower and *believe* the words as being true.

- **Manage stress.** There are many constructive ways to deal with the pressures of unemployment. Breathe deeply, listen to instrumental music, or focus on helping others.

- **Imagine a door-to-door salesperson.** Door-to-door salespeople know that they'll probably face a lot of rejection as they go knocking on doors trying to make sales. It may be weeks before they make a sale. But they hang in there and continue moving forward. *Remind yourself you're getting closer to your goal and it's the ultimate success that counts.*

- **Be confident.** Desperation works against you. Never appear desperate to have the job. Keep in mind that businesses are looking for candidates to solve their problems or issues. For instance, if you are applying to *McDonald's*, they may need someone who can handle heavy crowds at lunch time or in the evening or weekend; someone who can keep the line moving and fulfill orders accurately. Put your worries aside so you can make a good impression.

- **Remain active.** Continue searching as much as your time will allow. *Remember to tailor your resumes to the position. You may want to have several resumes if necessary. For instance, you may have a cashier resume which would be a little different from a stockroom resume. It's the same information but you will highlight the* *information relevant to the job you're applying for.* Rejection letters are easier to take if you're already looking ahead.

- **Refine your strategy.** If the job offer goes to someone else, you still get a chance to learn from the experience. Look for ways to become a stronger candidate.

Steps to Take in Specific Situations

- **Deal with pre-interview rejections.** If you're getting declined before an interview, it may indicate that you need to brush up your cover letter and resume. Double check your spelling and grammar and ensure you're using appropriate keywords. Ask someone with human resources experience to look over your documents.

- **Learn from your post-interview rejections. Try not to be disappointed. Use it as a learning tool to make your next interview better.** Maybe you're making it through multiple rounds of interviews before getting eliminated. You may want to rehearse more in advance to polish up your responses. Don't forget to send your thank you letters the same day or no later than the next day after your interview.

- **Get advice.** If you're new to the job market, rejections may come as a surprise. *Recent college graduates can take advantage of their campus* *career centers* to find resources on how to identify areas they need to work on.

- **Consider all your alternatives.** As a teen, also consider looking outside of the conventional job market. You may be able to baby sit, dog walk, rake leaves, sweep stores, run errands, shovel snow, etc. ***This could be the time to tap into your entrepreneurial and persuasion skills.***

- **Widen your search.** If you drive or are able to travel by bus or train, consider searching for work outside of your immediate area. Don't limit yourself to the jobs only in walking distance, unless you absolutely have to for personal or family reasons.

- **Review your qualifications.** If you're trying to apply for multiple different positions, it's important to determine if your background truly fits the needs of the position. You may find that additional training is required or that you need to clarify how your past accomplishments are relevant to the employer. Remember, don't send your cashier's resume to an employer looking for a stock person. Customize each resume to highlight the skills relevant to the job you're applying for to minimize rejection.

Each rejection brings you closer to the position that's right for you, so keep your spirits up and hang in there.

Learn to Handle Salary Discussions with Confidence

The most challenging part of a job interview for many candidates is the question of salary. *Being able to discuss money matters with confidence will help you get the compensation you want and may even improve your job satisfaction.* These are some steps to take before you get a job offer, after you get a job offer and in specific circumstances.

Steps to Take Before You Get a Job Offer

- **Let the interviewer bring it up first.** *It's always best to let the employer go first in any salary discussion.* Try to postpone discussing compensation until you receive a job offer. In some cases, especially in entry level positions, the salary or hourly rate will be disclosed during the interview. That way you have a better chance of staying in the running and negotiating with an employer who truly wants you on their team.

- **Assess your individual situation.** The exact approach you take will depend on the situation. You may be required to fill out an application stating your salary expectations. In that case, try naming a range rather than a specific figure.

- **Stress your interest in the position**. Let the person interviewing you know that you're enthusiastic about the company and the position. You don't have to jump for joy or do anything outrageous, but a well delivered verbal interest in the position lets the interviewer know that you're serious.

- **Background research.** Many employers conduct background searches on the employees they are considering for the position. With this in mind, never lie on a job application because it will probably be discovered and you could lose the job if hired or kill your chances of getting hired. Tell the truth about any incidents that may have happened previously and be ready to explain it. Simply state that you made a mistake, learned from it and intend to use it as a lesson going forward.

- Note: Remember never, and I mean *never* bad mouth a former employer or co-worker. If you speak negatively about a former company, it will only reflect poorly on you. The interviewer may conclude that you have an attitude problem, can't follow directions, are difficult to work with, not a team player or a host of other assumptions that will never be spoken. Bring out the positive traits of former jobs, even if you hated it.

Steps to Take After You Get a Job Offer

- **Ask for clarification.** Good job on receiving a job offer! You must have made quite an impression. Now is the time to discuss salary. It's still advantageous if you can get the employer to take the first step and let you know the budget they're working with. However, if they give you the option and ask you what kind of salary you're looking for, give them a range. For example, if you ask for $7 per hour and the position pays $9 per hour, you have just lost $2 per hour. They will not pay you $9 per hour if you only asked for $7 because it saves the company money.

  On the other hand, you don't want to price yourself out of a position by asking too much. So, if you're looking for $10 per hour, you can give a range of $8-$12 per hour. If you're on target with the salary, they will probably meet you in the middle and you'll get the $10. Every job is different, but always give a range, unless the salary was posted with the job description when you applied.

- **Be honest about your salary history.** Any salary information you provide may be verified, so tell the whole truth. Although, some employers only provide your title and time employed, you never know when your salary will be verified, so rather than take a chance and inflate it, just tell them the truth.

- **Negotiate in good faith.** Aim for a win-win solution. ***To start off on a good relationship with*** *your employer, you both want to feel that you were treated fairly. So don't say you're looking for $20 per hour when you know the job probably only pays about $12 per hour.*

Steps to Take in Special Circumstances

- **Juggle multiple offers skillfully.** If you have been using the strategies in this book and cleverly applying for many positions, you may be lucky enough to get more than one offer. Carefully weight which one you get the most benefit from, including location, salary, position, etc. After you have made your decision, give the employer a firm start date and graciously decline the 2nd option. You never want to burn bridges so be polite and thank them for the opportunity.

- **Interview for unpaid internships and volunteer jobs.** *Go ahead and check out n unpaid position that can give you more experience to beef up and diversify your resume.* You may be able to propose how you can be of extra value and wind up making you and your new boss very happy as well as open up possibilities for paid positions at a later date.

- **Consider taking a pay cut.** If you're faced with a difficult job search and you get an offer for a job that doesn't quite pay what you want, take it!

Something is better than nothing and you might be able to work your way up to a better salary in time.

Show up for your interview feeling ready and able to handle the question of compensation. Follow the techniques given and keep polishing your responses.

4 Tough Job Interview Questions and How to Answer Them

Congratulations on landing an interview for your dream job! *It's time to let your potential employer know why you're an outstanding candidate by finessing some tough, but typical, interview questions.*

Describing Your Setbacks or Weaknesses

While you're trying to impress the interviewer with your strengths, they'll naturally want to know about the areas where you still need to grow. Learn how to sound capable while talking about your weaker areas.

- **Be moderate.** Avoid anything so major that it would likely sink your chances of getting a job offer. Choose a flaw that's significant, but not a deal breaker. **Never say anything like "I can't stand when customers......" or "I hate when people....."** Anything negative like this will be a red flag to the interviewer and you will significantly decrease your chances of getting a job offer.

- **Focus on learning.** *Prove that you've learned from your past positions if you've had one.* For example, maybe you once gave a customer the wrong order. Simply say that after that experience, you were meticulous in checking the sales slip to ensure that the customer is getting the correct order.

- **Practice accountability.** Take responsibility for your performance. Your employer is eager to know that you'll be a team player, be responsible, stand behind your work and resolve issues as quickly as possible.

- **Refer to tasks that will play a small role in your work responsibilities.** For example, a cashier who struggles with typing raises less concern than one who has trouble counting money.

Discussing Your Greatest Achievements and Strengths

Talking about your assets in an interview can be a tricky situation because you want to seem extraordinary, without sounding conceited or arrogant.

- **Remain relevant.** Select qualities that are aligned with what they need. Let's say you are applying for a camp counselor position and your new boss is looking for someone who is active, vibrant and has a great disposition with kids, focus on your last camp counselor position and what you did to keep the kids engaged (if you actually had the job previously).

- **Tell vivid stories.** Create a personal connection by letting your enthusiasm and personality shine through. Provide details that show exactly how you handled a situation, solved a problem or contributed to a team project.

- **Distinguish yourself.** *You'll be more desirable for the position you're seeking if you can offer a unique benefit.* Maybe you're the only candidate who is bi-lingual or has a particular skill that could come in handy or be an asset to the position.

Negotiating Salary

Money talks can be tricky. A good strategy will keep you under consideration and be a win-win for both of you.

- **Preparing for salary negotiations.** Let your interviewer know if your requirements are flexible. You can do this by giving them a range like we spoke about earlier. Salary may be just one factor in your decision making. Consider the other benefits that matter to you, like location, hours, medical/dental, etc. Never let salary be the only determining factor in accepting a job offer.

  For instance, if you have a job offer for $10 per hour and is closer to home or school, versus a job that is several miles away and pays $15 per hour, you might want to carefully consider which of those positions will make you the best employee. You may not want to choose the job that is further away if you run the risk of being late consistently. Weigh all of your options carefully.

- **Back to salary ranges. When salary comes up, politely ask the interviewer if they can provide their salary range first.** However, if the interviewer insists on knowing your desired salary first, just give them the range that you had prepared.
- **Research salaries for similar positions.** Use the internet to find out what the going rate is for the job you're targeting. One website is www.salary.com. This knowledge will strengthen your bargaining position.

Posing Your Own Questions

Many interviews conclude with an invitation for you to ask your own questions. Posing thoughtful questions will make you more memorable and strengthen your case for being a good fit for the job. Prepare your questions beforehand if possible, otherwise, perhaps you have formulated a question after hearing about the position. Both are fine, but make it a well thought out question.

- **Revisit your strengths.** *Use your questions to summarize and recap your qualifications.* For example, asking about the company's social media contests could help you call attention to your experience with Facebook or Instagram campaigns.

- **Be courteous.** Watch for signs that the interviewer is looking to complete the session. Similarly, avoid subjects that could be controversial, like negative news stories about the company. It may be a sore subject, so leave it alone.

- **Is this really the job for you?** Determine if you truly want the position. While it's flattering to get any job offer, it's a better use of everyone's time to ascertain if this is a good fit for you. *Ask about the company's culture, training opportunities, and plans for growth.*

Respond to difficult interview questions with ease by rehearsing your answers in advance. You'll impress your potential new employer with your confidence and accomplishments.

Continue to use these strategies to convince interviewers that you're right for the job and you will increase your chances of getting multiple job offers right through your adult life. Don't worry. You got this!

Wishing you all the best!